She Says
Jennifer Murvin

Harbor Editions
Small Harbor Publishing

She Says
Copyright © 2024 JENNIFER MURVIN
All rights reserved.

Cover art and design: Maddy Cushman
Interior design: Kristiane Weeks-Rogers
Small Harbor Managing Editor: Kristiane Weeks-Rogers
Small Harbor Director: Allison Blevins

SHE SAYS
JENNIFER MURVIN
ISBN 978-1-957248-27-1
Harbor Editions,
an imprint of Small Harbor Publishing

For Ethan

"There is always another side, always."
—Jean Rhys

Contents

Ruffle / 13
after Robert Olen Butler

Crush / 21
after Kevin Brockmeier

Teacher's Assistant / 29
after Donald Barthelme

Gin in the Afternoon / 39
after Raymond Carver

Marble Halls / 49
after Tobias Wolff

Miss Emily, Poor Emily / 57
after William Faulkner

She Says

Foreword

This collection contains six rewrites of very famous, oft-anthologized short stories. These rewrites are an exercise in curiosity and close reading—encountering these stories again and again, I began to wonder what the (typically silent and/or secondary) women characters were thinking and experiencing. Each story is a reimagining of its original, a kind of creative criticism on one end and fan fiction on the other. For the fullest reading experience, you may wish to seek out the original stories.

The epigraph of this collection is from the writer Jean Rhys, who famously gave voice to Charlotte Brontë's "madwoman in the attic" in her novel *Wide Sargasso Sea,* a postmodern rewrite of *Jane Eyre.*

Ruffle
after Robert Olen Butler

> *She appeared in the den naked. I have not seen her naked since I fell from the tree and had no wings to fly . . . But now she appears from the hallway and I look at her and she is still slim and she is beautiful, I think—at least I clearly remember that as her husband I found her beautiful in this state. Now, though, she seems too naked. Plucked. I find that a sad thing . . . I want to pluck some of my own feathers, the feathers from my chest, and give them to her. I love her more in that moment, seeing her terrible nakedness, than I ever have before.*
> —Robert Olen Butler, "Jealous Husband Returns in Form of Parrot"

Parrots are so beautiful, I've always thought, like flirtatious women at a party, one drink in and all dressed up.

"Hello," I say to the parrot. It bows to me as if asking for a dance. "Pretty bird," I say. I want to speak its language. What a pleasure to look at birds in the middle of the day, with the smell of wood shavings and birdseed and stale pet food. "Hello," the parrot says back. My laugh is deep and sincere; it feels good to laugh this way. I will buy this bird as a pet, I will keep it and feed it. The power to make this decision feels as good as the laugh. Outside, the wet air of a Houston summer is not unlike a jungle.

"Pretty bird," I say again, because what if the bird missed it the first time?

"Whatcha got there?" Joe says. He doesn't let me too long in a store by myself. I want to say, "Whatya think I got, Joe, an armadillo?" but instead I say, "A parrot, of course."

His breath isn't good as he rests his chin on my shoulder, pokes his face bones into my skin. The parrot shrinks back a little.

"Quite a specimen," Joe says, loud enough for the young cashier to hear him. Joe doesn't talk to just one person, even when it's just him and me. It's like a camera is on him or something. "He talk?"

"He says, 'Hello.'" The parrot surely has more words it just isn't willing to share right now, which I respect.

Joe is circling the cage like shopping for a car.

"I want him," I say.

The cashier hears and comes over. "This is a yellow-nape Amazon. We call him Sammie."

Sammie is not the parrot's name, but I do not want to argue with the cashier. He is young with some pimples across his cheeks. He will be handsome one day, when he grows into himself. He will be strong. I imagine him with a woman, his face against hers, gentle with her hair.

"What do I need to buy?"

He speaks softly and when his voice lowers, Joe comes over and puts his hands around my waist. The parrot moves toward me also.

I buy the parrot toys, food, and a big black iron cage I can barely fit in the car. Joe thinks I'm *nuts*, but by that he means I'm sweet and cute—the way he says it makes me know this. I will put the parrot in the front room, by the window, so he can see the magnolias, so he can see velvety petals against the bright blue.

•

Yellow-nape Amazon parrots are named such for the yellow streak at the bottom of their necks. Otherwise, they are green as lush spring. They are green jewels or a mossy river in the morning. Their beaks are strong, and they like to chew. I bought Sammie (though I know that is not his name) toys and sometimes I watch him and he attacks a toy like his life depends on it. I want to chew something like my parrot chews his toys. I chew Joe this way, maybe, and I feel the urge to bite again.

•

    Things that don't fly: parrot toys, parrot seed, a man's pair of pants, a man.

•

    The parrot bites my neighbor's son when he puts his hand inside the cage.

    "I think he's jealous!" my neighbor says, laughing at her son.

    "Bad bird," the boy says.

    I suspect the boy pees on the toilet seat purposely before he leaves. My neighbor is very sweet; sometimes, she brings me baked goods made with coconut, my favorite.

    Later, I find a toy of the little boy's in the yard—an action figure—and I put it inside the birdcage for my parrot to play with. He leaves it alone, and eventually, I take the action figure out of the cage and throw it in the trash.

•

    Yellow-nape Amazon parrots are known for "nest-protective behaviors." But if something can leave the parrot's nest, is it part of the nest at all? Surely there is a difference between the nest itself and the things that live in the nest? I imagine my parrot, with his gray feet like a dinosaur's, guarding his nest with historical impulse, his voice repeating, "Hello." In Hawaiian, the same word means *Hello* and *Goodbye*, which might be confusing, though economical.

•

    One day, I leave the door of the cage open to see what he'll do. He flies out and right into the glass door. His little head hits the glass with a terrible noise, and I think: I have killed him.

But he is just stunned. His feathers move, and I pick him up in my hand, and he is as light as a coconut flake. Against my chest, I imagine I can feel his heart fluttering. What did I think was going to happen, leaving the door open? I am as cruel as a word that can mean both itself and its opposite. When I weep, my tears fall onto my parrot's green feathers, and they take on a look of a swamp at dusk. In Houston, swamps have alligators, which are also green—though they have teeth, and my parrot only a beak, which he does not open to say anything as I hold him, his tiny body fragile and shimmering.

•

Later, when I tell Grant what I want him to do to me, when I listen for his accent thick as an Amazon summer, when I climb his tall body like a palm, I am aware of my parrot down the hall, his cage door closed. I hear a tinkle of a bell, and I know he is attacking his toy again, that satisfying release. Grant thinks the sound is a wind chime, and he says he'd like to get some for his porch.

Grant likes to walk around half naked, and I admire his body for what it can do to mine, for how he holds it with the foundation of his cowboy boots. When Grant walks past the cage, the parrot calls after him, "Cracker." Cracker! Oh, dear. "Hello, cracker!" the parrot calls again.

"Funny little thing," Grant says, his mouth against my neck as he winds a hand up my skirt, and I think what a pleasure it is to be a woman in her own home.

"Pretty bird," the parrot calls, and I'm glad he's cheering himself up, but all I can hear now is Grant's breath in my ear and my own moans.

•

Things that cannot fly: wind chimes, an iron cage, a glass door, a man's shoe, a man.

•

My neighbor once told me a story about her little boy, that she had threatened to take a toy from him when he was disobedient in the car, and that he had himself thrown the toy out of the backseat window, preferring to destroy the thing itself before someone else could take it away.

We clasped each other's hands a bit, after that story, she telling it, me hearing.

•

It is not lost on me that the color for jealousy is green, though I imagine jealousy green is not a pretty green like my parrot's feathers, which shine in the sunlight that comes through the glass door like something you could fly through (but you can't). A house without children is called an empty nest, but what about a house without a husband?

•

Things that fall out of trees: acorns, seeds, green husbands, baby parrots who do not yet know how to fly.

•

After Grant is asleep (such a tall, strong man, my Grant—I like him so much more than Joe, and I can't wait to hear his accent again in the morning), I walk naked into the living room to see what the parrot is up to. I want a snack and in this second life, I no longer deny myself when I want something.

"Hello," says the parrot.

I walk into the kitchen and the air from the refrigerator cools my bare stomach. There is fruit and cheese.

"Hello" says the parrot.

He really is a darling little pet. I'm so glad his head survived that hit to the glass.

"Pretty bird," he says. His eyes are doing the funny thing they do. "Eye pinning," this is called, when a parrot expands and contracts his pupils. A sign of stress or excitement.

Did I think the waiter was handsome, my dead/fallen husband wanted to know, why was I looking at the cashier, how long had I spent with the electrician, what was this smell on the sheet? I wonder, what if the neighbor's little boy had chosen to throw his mother out of the window instead of his toy? Soon, the little boy will be a man.

Green, a pretty color, I think, but not beautiful! I ring the parrot's little bell, but he does not attack.

"Pretty," the parrot says.

"Bad," he says.

"Open," he says, and I open his door. My sweet little parrot, I am so glad I bought him. What do people do without pets? A person needs something to care for.

"Up," he says, like a child. I reach in and he climbs into my hand, spindly naked feet on my naked fingers.

I imagine for a moment my parrot as a little poet with only a few words available to him, a prompt, a restriction meant, ultimately, to free up the creative mind!

Sometimes, there is a danger to imagining a story that isn't true, the biggest danger being imagining it so much you make it so.

"Poor baby," I say to my parrot, who is trembling against my hand. I want him to be free, like me, but his little claws dig in so tight. If I plucked his feathers, I could make a crown, I could make earrings, I could adorn a hat.

"Poor baby," he echoes. And I think: those are my poetry words, go get your own.

"Bad bird," he says.

I want to tell him, *Stop accusing yourself and everyone else*. A bird cannot be bad any more than a man can fly out of a tree. Soon, my neighbor's little boy will have no toys left, and what will occupy his time then?

Grant walks in, his boots on and nothing else. He likes to make me laugh. He doesn't mind that I taste like fruit, that maybe I have left none for him.

"Peanut," says my parrot, and we laugh, because it's funny, a parrot asking for a peanut when we have none.

"Hello," the parrot says as we walk away, but does he mean *Goodbye*? The parrot talks some more, his words as confusing as a door made of glass, but I no longer hear him as I am entering a jungle of my own. Grant's boots are off and so am I, into a bed that is not a nest but a sky.

Crush

after Kevin Brockmeier

It occurred to me that if nothing were to change, if the ceiling were simply to hover where it was forever, we might come to forget that it was ever there, charting for ourselves a new map of the night sky.
—Kevin Brockmeier, "The Ceiling"

We have about six inches left, I'd say. Can you measure time in inches? We can. A drowning person might look up at the inches of water between her nose and the surface. A person with her head under an axe. This is the time she has left. Six inches tick tock tick tock tick tock five.

Does the punishment fit the crime? It does not, but I understand there is no such thing as fairness. I understand the difference between a sky and a ceiling, no need for a demonstration! My nose will go first. My lips. Eyes. Chin. Teeth, I've always had a bit of an overbite. Then my breasts. My belly next. The rest. I hope the soil doesn't accept me, I couldn't handle a sinking. Six inches, I haven't bargained for more.

If I'm honest, I don't know what love is except for my baby.

At first, I just liked to watch Mitch mow his lawn. Mitch, our neighbor. My husband hired our lawn out; he never cut the grass on the land we owned. I dug the flower garden. Did that count? I had not argued about the hired lawn mowing, which seemed to me a man's domain.

What does that say about me? But then again, I went for the man who did mow his lawn: Mitch. Our neighbor. Blond like a sunrise, like a morning sun through a window, like a little girl's hair. Which is a strange comparison, but I do feel protective of him, as if his blondness makes him vulnerable, like a child. When he first kissed me, he tasted like sunscreen, which I found responsible.

Darling Mitch, who lies now with his stomach five, four inches from the ceiling; he is larger than me, and so it will take less time for the crushing to begin, for him. It does seem poetic, poetic justice even: adulterers, punished by the sky itself. The whole world exacting moral vengeance. It feels Biblical, but I understand I am no Jesus, or even Judas. I have no such agenda or belief. Who would pay attention to me, a woman born and raised in the Ozarks to marry a man and birth a child and sleep with a neighbor and bring the end of the world? Not that I'm taking responsibility, not that I have hubris—but the metaphor is damning. I cannot help but think of myself as a symbol. I know guilt like I know my palm. Like I know my heartbeat, like I know my child's eyelashes patterning his cheeks at bedtime.

Mitch. Blond hair, big chest, his small round ass rising above strong thighs. When he climbs on top of me, I die quietly inside. His green eyes take my world from me—I am no longer a mother, a wife—I am just a body, a woman's body, made to receive him. And it is glorious, this exit from myself into myself. Punishment for this? Crushing by sky. The ceiling, they call it now, which is a more appropriate word, in that the sky has become not infinity opening into space but a hard shell overhead. *The ceiling is descending*, the man says on the news while he cries cries cries, and my son says, "Mommy?" His way of asking me to explain. "Mommy?" he asks. Which means, "What? Why?" I have no answer for my boy. *How dare you!* the ceiling says. *And with the neighbor, you common whore!*

Who's to say who started it? I could say I did not like my husband anymore, which was true, but whose fault was this? Had he grown unlikeable, or had I grown unable to like him? We were so young when we got married, with young ideas of dressing up and wearing rings. In the shadow of the ceiling, the question of blame insists even as it will become irrelevant.

Between questions is the answer that is Mitch, who cut his own grass, who said I looked beautiful in my pink tank top, who said I reminded him of his favorite aunt, who said my cookies were the best cookies he'd ever had, who said he'd never have thought of cranberries and white chocolate—what a combo, lady! Who had taken his tongue to me for the first time underneath the apple tree in the backyard during late morning, telling me I smelled like bliss and tasted like heaven; and who knew a man could want a woman so very badly, as he wanted me, right then, under the apples and sky which was not a ceiling then but blue space where anything could happen, home to birds or stars or rocket ships or balloons floating up like wishes.

The first sign of the ceiling arrived the night of my son's sixth birthday. Selfishly, I felt my son's birthday to be my own special day—the anniversary of the day I had given birth to him, the day I had let go of my heart inside to out, given it fully to the chaos and violence of the world, invited the chaos and violence in, really, into the space just recently vacated by my tiny son who had begun that day his steady (but natural, but natural) process of leaving me. I had felt a surrender to my own body as a place of loss—inevitable, I saw then—I was complicit and also damned. His frail body was yellow with jaundice; he sat under a lamp like a plant, like a lizard, while I made notes: eyelashes like delicate, frayed branches; wrinkled fingers; nails thin and translucent with magical ephemeral pink; belly distended with hunger—for me! Oh, the details, the notes, the first lines of the story of the crush. Thin lips sucking, a little crust stuck to his boney shoulder, squirming legs seeking my walls and finding only open air.

The sixth anniversary of this, my son's birthday, and what was I doing? That day, I was a little drunk on a margarita, letting my toe hook onto the leg of Mitch's folding chair, the only way I could get close to him as my husband looked on. My husband loved me, then. I knew, even when he left for the bars (am I dropping this detail to defend myself? to whom? for what?), that he loved me. He sang us to sleep some nights, me and our son. He had cried over our naked bodies in the birthing room.

My husband is not evil or a villain, though he dies, too, in this story. Collateral damage, as is my son. If they didn't die, if it were only me and my lover to meet our squishy end, the story would be a comedy, and this story is not a comedy. In that story, the story that is a comedy, my husband would be the hero. This story has no hero, except maybe the ceiling, which one can't help but admire as something bold and beautiful, manifested metaphor, proof of an Artiste, capital A—italics even. (Who else but an *Artiste* could manufacture such perfect ironies? It is beautiful, the tidiness, like Mitch's perfect mowed rows on his perfect green lawn, perfect teeth, perfect tongue.)

They do not tell you, the women who are around you, the mothers, your mothers, how it is to see your baby with his eyelashes sleeping at night. His little body, how easily a bookshelf could come over onto him, how likely! this will happen on your watch, how the cord from the blind could strangle him, how easily he could drown, how easily he could drown even after you have believed that he hasn't drowned—they don't tell you about second drowning, inhaled water into the lungs to drown your baby in his sleep just as you have gone to bed thinking, yes, thank you God, I have kept him alive another day. They do not tell you how you will dream of hot cars suffocating him while you grocery shop in a sleepy daze, your baby forgotten by you in his car seat which you chose specially for its safety rating; they do not tell you about the dogs who bite the sun which burns the grapes the hot dogs the cherry tomatoes that choke choke choke, will choke your baby while you are watching because you forgot, you unfit whore of a mother, sleeping with her neighbor, unhappy with her husband, radiant with sex or love or sex and love, to cut those grapes, tomatoes, hot dogs, and shouldn't your baby be eating organic spinach anyway, yes he should.

  How quickly I realized there was no luxury for mistakes as a mother, no place in the body with its empty room for a blip in memory, in attention, in focus, in anticipation. The perfect environment for the most careless mistakes of all—careless and maybe even purposeful as a woman who is told she can't fly will jump off a building to show you her wings, which do not exist.

  Of course, the birds have all gone away now.

  There is no sky, only ceiling.

  It is a classic story, Kate Chopin mastered it after all. A woman who crushes will be henceforth crushed.

  The question: Is she freed or is she simply dead?

  I know no dead people, so I have no one to ask. My husband says he has imagined his dead parents on the other side of the ceiling—he says one can only imagine a ceiling here is a floor somewhere else, which makes logical sense to me. I found his parents to be very sweet if not traditional in the sense that they called each other "Mother" and "Father." "Mother, will you pass the sugar?" my father-in-law would ask my mother-in-law, who would then pass it, with a shy smile. If our ceiling is their floor, we will certainly not hear them dancing or making a ruckus in the way of more interesting neighbors.

If Mitch and I are reborn, karma dictates we will continue to pay for our crimes. My little son said once, he'd like to try on the life of our cat. I wish him to return as a cat, but a domesticated one, content with a window to look at birds, which would, in his next life, return in great murmurations. I wish him a sky with no ceiling. I wish him a bowl of cold water and sneaks of roast chicken from a loving child who dotes on him endlessly, if not suffocatingly, as is the way with small children and pets.

What is the connection between my son and my lover? Perhaps it is power, or lack thereof; I am a desperate woman, loose in the sky like my son's birthday balloons on the last birthday he would have where there would be a sky for balloons to fly in. My ribbon was cut—my husband cut it in the hospital delivery room; I watched him do it. "Would you like to cut the cord?" the doctor asked him, as if this part of my body wasn't mine anymore. No one asked me would I like it cut, would I like to cut it—my own body from my own body. My husband cut it, gleefully, while the nurse snapped a photo. Large and small cuts, before the crush, like you might prep a potato for boiling. Easier to skin the potato after, before the mashing.

Inches left.

Somehow we are lying together—Mitch, me, my husband. My boy and Mitch's boy at our feet, asleep like cats or angels. Effortless and fierce. Please let them sleep through it, gentle, like no one I have ever known has died—*in their sleep*—my little son and I have a game where we plan to meet in our dreams, the ice cream shop, the diner with the pancakes. *See you there, I'll meet you there, see you soon.*

"Do you ever get the feeling that you're supposed to be someplace else?" I ask.

My little son will order blue ice cream with the little chunks of cake in it. Me, rocky road. There, the ceiling is decorated with stickers shaped like stars. Rainbows with glitter. Lanterns dangle like jewelry. "It's like a kind of dread."

"Worth it," whispers Mitch into my ear, and if the ceiling would allow me the freedom of movement to do it, I'd spit in his beautiful eyes.

My husband takes my hand and moves it to his mouth. His lips are wet against my skin. He massages my hand like trying to wring water from a stone.

Cruelly, I find the ceiling reflecting my own face, and I watch myself come closer, lowering, lowering, as for a kiss.

Teacher's Assistant
after Donald Barthelme

> *And they said, is death that which gives meaning to life? And I said no, life is that which gives meaning to life. Then they said, but isn't death, considered as a fundamental datum, the means by which the taken-for-granted mundanity of the everyday may be transcended in the direction of–I said, yes, maybe.*
> —Donald Barthelme, "The School"

I had hope for the new school. The morning I was hired as the teacher's assistant, a ladybug landed on my windowsill while I was washing dishes. I looked at the clock the moment it hit 8 a.m. on the nose. My hair curled under. All these things spelled *Hope*.

We'd started out strong. "Helen," the teacher said, "you're a life saver," because before he'd come into the classroom that first day I'd organized the children's cubbies, checked off their homework and recorded it in the little gradebook, and tidied the reading corner with books by theme: love, loss, coming of age, slapstick humor, activity, mystery, adventure, romance. I was the early bird and all that jazz. The teacher was a handsome man, I liked his orange hair and white eyebrows. He reminded me of a creamsicle.

Had I references? Why, yes I had—four references in all from various schools in which I'd gained valuable experience. I owned many sticker books. The children brought me flowers in springtime, stems wrapped in foil, and baked me homemade cupcakes with sprinkles. I'd assembled garlands made of cards and letters written in crayon declaring my students' LUV, 4ever.

The teacher, with me assisting, began a new unit on photosynthesis. I started it all by recommending orange trees—I can see this now. How I made it happen again. I'd loved orange trees since I was a girl growing up in Valencia, California, the city named for the orange named for the city (in Spain). Valencia oranges are sweet. Preferable for juice-making, full of Vitamin C, healthy for the skin and the prevention of scurvy. Oranges are often left in Christmas stockings to represent the bags of gold given by St. Nicholas to pay for the girls' dowries in the famous legend. Think of the husbands we could buy!

When I cut myself shaving my legs that morning and orange juice came out in lieu of regular blood (a terrible stinging, you can't imagine), I had a sinking feeling the trees were dead.

In the plot of garden beside the schoolyard, the teacher looked at me with desperate eyes. "How sad," he said. "Like little graves." He was right—the lifeless sticks stood in rows like photos I'd seen of Arlington. The children danced around them; the sticks were lightsabers, emerging up from tombs of zombie Jedis. They were so creative, these children! I loved them dearly.

Mother had said Jordan left her because of the kitten, which was code for because of me. When she cried at the kitchen table, I quietly rearranged the plastic plants. Mother's left eye was going blind; she glared at me with her right. Blindness doesn't affect tear production. Mother would be happy I had found a good job at another school. She would be happy to hear about the books arranged by theme: space, feelings, friendship, invisible friends, how-to.

"Mother," I said on a voicemail, "did you ever think that chloroplasts look a little like dirty plastic kiddie pools? I miss you."

The frozen snakes had been an accident; winter was hard on reptiles, especially those kept in rooms made of concrete. I was brand new to the school those days, hardly involved with the children at all. I only knew the names of the troublemakers and the ones with pushy mothers. Poor snakes! It was my great grieving that caused me to hear only words beginning with "s" for several days following.

"Something," the teacher said. "Strikes strikes started strikes." Poor snakes! Always the villains. An interesting exercise, I thought, in alliteration. I used it in a lesson later. A good teacher seizes every opportunity to teach.

Jordan's kitten had breath that smelled like mint, because she was forever eating the mint leaves in the neighbor's yard. The day the kitten didn't make it, I vomited mint leaves into the toilet, and Jordan saw when he was cleaning up after me. Jordan had been the only man my mother loved, she said. (She didn't talk about my father except for how he died.) Jordan had hands like paws. Fingers like magic. He knew a poem or two by heart and didn't mind sleeping only four hours a night. Mother said Jordan was a machine. She said Jordan fixed the water heater and saved her $400 during a very rough Christmas, a very rough Christmas. Jordan had loved the kitten, had named the kitten after his dead grandmother, even. And then I vomited up the mint leaves. There were other things. The mint was the Bombe. That was the name of the famous British codebreaker machine, which did battle against the German encryption machine called Enigma. Following the comparison here, this would make me Enigma. When Jordan left, Mother drove us to the ocean and put me in a hotel by the beach but not on the beach, and she told me not to talk to anyone. She left me there for two nights, but she gave me money and said I could order as much pizza as I wanted, and to make sure I drank plenty of water. I watched as much TV as I could before my eyes turned red. Mother came back with her left eye half-blind and said that was her punishment and she'd take it for two days of peace, goddamn it.

The children drowned the herb garden in their eagerness. It is not attractive to be smothered, this can even lead to death. Just ask my boyfriend two boyfriends ago, I wanted to say, but did not as we had not yet reached the unit on Safety. Another lesson shortly after: Don't carry small animals (salamanders) around in plastic baggies. Was this school Montessori? Maybe it was. The teacher cried only for the suffocated amphibian. (Not so for the sunken basil, which had made my own eyes tickle.) His white lashes were so wet with tears, they looked unworldly. I longed to lick them dry. "The children," the teacher said. "How much more can they take?"

Mother was careful to avoid the neighbors, to arrange rocks in the garden, to just say no to the Girl Scouts, dear God, out there amongst the bears. She denied my grandparents access—my father's mother hated her anyway, she said, because she blamed my mother for my father's death just weeks after my conception (Mother did the math). He'd driven the car off the bridge and into the ocean. His car had filled with water before he could get out. His mother had apparently thought my mother overworked him, pestered him at night to listen to her read all her poems aloud, to offer support and carefully worded criticism. Mother told me this story to teach me not to drive on bridges over water. Mother sometimes missed Jordan so much she'd wander around the house stripping down to her underwear, slowly. "Come out, come out, wherever you are." Jordan never came out because he had moved back to Arizona where maybe mint didn't grow.

"Mother," I said into her voicemail, "I'm on break soon and I would like to see you." Mother never called me back, but I suspected this was because she was spending her days trying to find Jordan again, searching canyons.

Could I have suspected the consequence of my vacation plans to Hawaii? Viewing the dead tropical fish belly up like sunbathing soccer moms, I couldn't help but feel responsible. I would not snorkel to atone.

I do not want to talk about the puppy. Its only mistake was to let me name it after a famous author. Edgar. Mother had read me "The Tell-Tale Heart" when I was little; "Was it possible they heard not? Almighty God! --no, no! They heard! --they suspected! --they knew! --they were making a mockery of my horror!" I read it aloud to the children, who loved the part about the dismembering—how children love the grotesque! The teacher was growing thinner, his cheekbones more pronounced. His freckles were glorious, his skin like homemade vanilla cupcakes with sprinkles.

Mother said it was her fault, that one time in grad school after a bad workshop she'd smoked too much pot and made a wish on an eclipse that she'd have something to write about forever. She said sometimes she'd like to stab me with a fork, think of everyone she could save, but she was no Abraham. She often compared our situation to Biblical stories and various mythologies; literature, she said, is full of torment against women and the punishment of artists. Mother was a big reader, but she never let me go to the library after I had snuck into her copy of *Jane Eyre*—the fire had burned up the whole nonfiction section and hurt a man who had been napping under Self-Help and Relationships. Mother said everyone knows to sleep in the bathroom.

She took me to the woman at the shop in the valley with the sign that said Palm Readings and Suntanning. She took me to a woman in a brick building downtown who lit things and chanted and maybe there was blood, but Mother said it was fake, could I smell it?, and this woman should be put in jail and Mother could never get that $50 back, no she would not. These shopkeepers didn't have a cure for the Enigma that was me. She took me to a man who'd had an advertisement in the paper. He had credentials, Mother said, and an office in Santa Monica we had to take an elevator up to, but Mother took me back down the elevator very quickly after he'd asked to speak to her privately in his office, and when I asked her why we were leaving, she said she'd like me to think about the man hard that night as I went to sleep. She wrote his name down on a piece of paper for me to look at.

"Mother," I told her voicemail. "Mother. Mother? Come out, come out, wherever you are."

Mother had read Poe to me so dramatically, standing up and slamming her tall heavy heels against the linoleum of the kitchen floor: "I could bear those hypocritical smiles no longer! I felt that I must scream or die! and now --again! --hark! louder! louder! louder! louder!"

The children had been taught well by the movies they watched and were less fazed by the human losses that came soon after the trees, snakes, mice, gerbils, and salamander. Yes, they had written the adopted international student who lived in Korea letters about American culture, asking after the way he did things instead. Over *there*. He had been serious in his responses and his drawings a little too excellent for comfort. He had cost each of them a quarter per month, the same as a gumball.

It was The School, everyone was thinking, no one turning their eyes to me, the teacher's assistant, my apartment perched atop a Korean restaurant that made the best fish egg stew I'd ever had, the stew I'd eaten for dinner every night since I moved to town.

At night, I dreamed of orange trees, but instead of oranges, the branches were laden with little suns, and instead of seeds, there were fish eggs, and when the eggs hatched, they turned into puppies who barked warnings I couldn't understand because the puppies weren't Lassie, they were all famous authors, ones whose stories had morals.

When the parents died, I let the children snot on my good black dress. Grandparents fell like dominoes.

Two boys from the school were crushed by lumber while playing at a construction site one evening after school. I was asleep at the time, a little drunk on champagne, to tell you the truth. Splinters can be removed, I found out, by soaking your hands in warm water and then using sharp tweezers or even a needle to extract the wood. You can sterilize the tweezers and needles with an open flame.

I only wanted to show Billy the mask and knife I had bought on my trip to South America; he was to report the next week on Nicaragua. His father had died, of course, murdered by a man wearing the same mask and carrying the same knife. Well, not the same, but similar. Of course. This, being all of it. Every time. If only they'd known about the mint! But they didn't have the Bombe, not like Jordan did—too late for his poor kitten, but early enough for him to plan his own escape. Poor Mother. Billy's father had not bled orange juice, because that would have been ridiculous.

Jordan's kitten was gray with black stripes and a breath of mint, and I would hold her up to my face to smell it. The kitten's whiskers had tickled my cheeks, and her eyes were like photos of galaxies I'd seen in science books, and I loved her like maybe Mother had loved Jordan—like not breathing, like consuming, like draw the kitten a million times in the notebook just to spend time with her tiny kitten face, the lesson being those short lifespans of pets and orchids and Jordans and other things precious and worthy of our attention and grief.

The children wanted to know, where did they go? The dead animals, children, parents, grandparents, friends? The teacher didn't know. His voice was strangled. Poor teacher! How cruel of the children, to expect him to know everything! It wasn't fair. He tried so hard—he wore t-shirts with the school's name on Spirit Fridays. He led assemblies and organized a dance themed to Elvis. Who knew what happened to the dead things, then? Nobody, he said. His school T-shirt was wet in the armpits. I could wash it, hang it to dry on a line hung across the backyard, iron it crisp as an apple.

I was only the assistant, which meant I didn't have to answer the hard questions. I refilled the glue in case the children got hungry.

I looked out the window toward where the herb garden had been before the children had loved it to death. Had we finished the unit on photosynthesis? We had moved on to precipitation. There was something to the idea of cycles. Later, I might draw a diagram. We read "The Raven" for literature; when we asked the children to line up after recess, they'd call out to us from the swings, "Nevermore!"

I listened again when the children used my name. Helen. They wanted the teacher to make love to me. They demanded what could only be called an education. Oh, children! They were ready to graduate, their bodies tiny in robes and caps. They would take over the world.

The children watched while I moved to the teacher and put my arms around his strong body. He smelled like basil or mint, a jaunty afternoon cocktail. He quivered and kissed my forehead like a father, like a priest. I pressed my hips to his. I waited for the next lesson he would teach us.

Gin in the Afternoon
after Raymond Carver

> *We could have been anywhere, somewhere enchanted. We raised our glasses again and grinned at each other like children who had agreed on something forbidden.*
> —Raymond Carver, "What We Talk About When We Talk About Love"

Nick's friend Mel was talking. Mel is a cardiologist, maybe he liked to talk so much because he couldn't talk when his hands were inside someone's chest. Maybe because he'd saved those urgent words that came to him on the beat of someone else's heart, and the words had been rising to the surface all this time since.

Mel preached. Nick, my husband, was amused by this mostly. He was feeling warm toward me. He admired Mel's profession.

The four of us—Nick, me, Mel, and Mel's wife Teresa—sat in their sunny kitchen drinking gin. I prefer red wine. Red wine is better for the heart. Resveratrol reduces low-density lipoprotein which helps prevent blood clots. Teresa was called Terri. Terri was Mel's second wife. I wouldn't remember the first because I never met her, but Terri spoke of her often. Every time we got up to the sink to wash, Terri would talk about Mel's first wife. Mel's first wife never did the dishes. Mel's wife had sex fully clothed. Mel's wife adopted one of the lion mothers at the zoo. One might mistake Terri talking about Mel's first wife as Terri talking about her own deceased mother with whom she'd had a complicated relationship.

It was afternoon, early for drinking. Mel was talking about love: real love, which was spiritual love. He'd gone to seminary, he'd learned about God—which is to say, he'd learned about love. This was before he'd learned about hearts.

Terri said the man she'd lived with before Mel had loved her so much he'd tried to kill her. She said he'd dragged her around the room, saying, "I love you. I love you, you bitch." She looked at everyone. Terri was thin and dark, with a long face, like Cher. She wore bright turquoise jewelry, and I thought maybe I should wear more jewelry, maybe it would light me up.

Terri's neck was so slender, I could wrap my hands around it very easily. Nick had called me a bitch once. I couldn't remember why, only the shape of it coming out of his mouth. He does not often curse. I must have done something pretty awful.

Mel didn't think this was love. That man of Terri's had caused them a lot of grief, he said, threatening Mel, calling him up at the hospital to say violent things. Mel had bought a gun, he was so scared.

Terri said the man might have acted crazy, but there was no doubt he loved her. I didn't know if I agreed, so I stayed silent, gin on my tongue. (A useless alcohol. I could feel no effect on my lipoprotein whatsoever.) Was Terri a romantic? She seemed to reflect on the man fondly. Or maybe the situation more than the man. She was worth killing for, dying for. This maybe had classical implications?

When Mel reached across the table to touch Terri's face, I felt something turn over in my belly.

"Now he wants to make up," she said. Mostly that phrase reminded me of *make believe*.

Mel liked to talk about love, she said. The name of Terri's man came to me: Ed. Terri had talked about him once, how she had bought him everything in the house: his mattress, the TV, the coffee table, the dishware. She had gone into incredible debt and was still paying it off. She'd told me she'd paid for Ed's gun, that Mel could never know this. She could trust me, right?

She could trust me.

Nick said he didn't know if this sounded like love, but he thought what Mel was saying is that love is absolute.

Nick only knew about love from songs, I wanted to say, but I didn't. Besides, how could that be true? And what kind of woman would say that about her new husband?

I said I didn't know anything about the situation, and how could anyone judge?

Nick touched my hand; he liked when I was easygoing in a crowd. Restful, he'd said once. I tried to live up to it, and mostly did. He ran his fingers over my nails; I'd painted them to keep from biting. I longed for something between my teeth. In some cultures, people with weak hearts were fed the strong hearts of other animals.

Terri went on—it was like she couldn't stop. The man, Ed, had eaten rat poison when she'd left him. Like the Faulkner story, except Ed fed the poison to himself, and he hadn't died. All his gums rotted.

There was more; I was waiting for the gun to go off. Sure enough, he'd shot himself in the mouth, but he'd bungled that, too. Terri's word: *bungle*. Poor Ed. Terri's words, again.

Mel had no sympathy for Ed, but it is only that he couldn't compete.

It should go without saying—no one had loved Mel, Nick, or me like that. That was what Terri was accusing, and we were guilty.

What happened after he bungled it? I wanted to know, leaning forward. The gin was working; I had to prop myself up on my elbows. I held my glass between my hands like a prayer.

•

What had happened? Mel said someone in the apartment complex heard the shot and went to investigate. Mel had been at the hospital when Ed had been brought in—his head swollen up twice the size of a normal head. I tried to imagine this and could only find it funny, but tears came instead. Terri had wanted to sit with Ed. Mel hadn't wanted her to do this. Terri won, of course. No one doubted she had the power. She sat with Ed, he had no one else. He died without waking up.

Ed, Ed, the Giant Head. Ed the Giant Head is Dead.

Had she sung him to sleep? Recited a poem? Told him she loved him, that he had finally won? Won her?

He had no mouth left to tell her anything, in the end. The rat poison ate his gums, then he'd shot his teeth off to finish the job. In the Faulkner story, Emily feeds her lover rat poison so she can kill him and sleep next to his dead body for years and years. Was this love? Real, spiritual, absolute?

Mel reclined back in his chair like a man at the lake. "I'm not interested in that kind of love. If that's love, you can have it."

She did have it, and Mel didn't. This was obvious. Would Terri hang herself by her turquoise necklace for Mel? Don't bet on it. Mel's first wife had said, "Okay," when Mel told her he was leaving her for Terri. This reaction was legendary. "Okay," Mel's first wife had said. Then she took all the money.

I met Nick at the law office where I work as a secretary. He is a caterer. He gave me a whole cheesecake when he left the office; it had been meant for the partners' Christmas dinner. I ate the cheesecake over a week for breakfast each morning. We had both been married before, and no kids was the official story.

Terri poured the last of the gin and Mel got another bottle down from the cabinet.

•

"Nick and I know what love is," I said. "For us, I mean." What I should have said was, we know what love isn't. As I said, we had both been married. Once I forgot what my ex-husband's name was; we had been married for eight years.

Nick took my hand and kissed it loudly, I could feel his tongue licking my skin, cold from the gin and tonic. I didn't like the feeling, but I didn't want to draw my hand back. I loved Nick.

"We're lucky," I said.

They exclaimed, Terri and Mel, we were in the honeymoon phase; we were making them sick. Terri said, "Wait a while." Her dark eyes were looking through me—maybe Ed was standing behind me, at the window, waiting to shoot Mel at last.

"I'm only kidding," she said.

Mel came around with the bottle, toasting, he said, to true love!

•

Albuquerque is windy this time of year. I could hear Mel and Terri's trees scratching against the side of the house. The Sandia Mountains rose somewhere outside; Mel and Terri's house disoriented me. We were in the middle of the basin, this I knew. *Sandia*: watermelon. Watermelon might taste lovely mixed with gin. Everything goes with red wine. I missed Missouri in the spring, pink and white dogwoods mixing their blooms, tulip magnolias, pink as fingernail beds. A solid thunderstorm. A dog barked. The sun felt like it was shining from inside the kitchen. I yearned for sunglasses.

Nick was smiling; I hadn't seen him so content in months. He was mischievous, drunk before dark on a weekday.

"I'll tell you what real love is," said Mel.

Nick put his hand on my knee, which was bare. My shorts were too tight, pressing into my belly.

Nick was a chef who catered; you'll remember this is how we met. I loved his food, the way it filled me up. The way it tasted on my tongue. "Make me . . ." I would say, filling in whatever I craved. Donut. Enchilada. Fried chicken. Mango salsa. My favorite was when he'd bring his food to my mouth with his own fingers. I had grown a bit fatter in the last eighteen months. Rounder. Nick squeezed me when we had sex, and I found this satisfying and erotic.

My ex-husband (what was his name again?) hadn't understood when I lost the baby. The doctor—it had not been Mel, though the condition had been more heart-related than anything else—said kindly that a miscarriage was often a private grieving between the woman and her baby. The doctor had said this like she knew how it was. She held my hand; she said it was for the best. Maybe the baby would have been sick or deformed. She said I had rescued myself. I had loved the baby, and my body had killed it. Was this love? Spiritual or scientific?

I wasn't listening to Mel, his voice droning like a bee.

"Are you drunk, honey?" Terri said. "Are you drunk?"

Mel was handsome, trim and tan from playing tennis.

"I'm not on call today!" he said. So many hearts, waiting on him. Where were his hands? the wind seemed to ask on their behalf.

"Mel, we love you," I said, speaking also for the hearts.

He didn't recognize me, which was understandable.

"Love you too, Laura," he said, like saying goodbye. "You too, Nick. You guys are our pals." He toasted again without the words. He wanted to tell us another story—something, he said, that would make us ashamed of talking about love.

Terri protested. Be quiet, he said. Or maybe it was shut up. Shut up for once in your life.

But would a man say that to a woman he loved?

The story was this: Once upon a time, an old man and an old woman, husband and wife, drove a camper. Once upon a time, a teenager got drunk and drove his father's pickup. These characters meet on the road. The teenager dies; he is the villain, being drunk. The old couple lives, because they are wearing their seatbelts, and because they are in love. This is a moral, children.

"I love you, hon," Terri said, amused by the seatbelts.

"Honey, I love you," he said back.

They kissed across the table; it was loud and I didn't like the noise.

The story continued: The old couple is taken to the hospital, as is the boy, even though the boy is dead. The doctors—Mel included—work on the couple for hours. They live. They survive ICU. They are beaten, not broken. Soon, they get their own room.

Mel stopped the story. He and Terri wanted to take us to dinner, to a new place. Though I was hungry, I was more hungry for the old couple, for what had happened to them. I drank up my gin. It was awful stuff, really, even the lime didn't help it. I ran the lime across my lips. Nick would like that, I thought, the surprise of a lime there.

Maybe thinking of Nick, Mel said in another life he'd want to be a chef. Maybe thinking of Ed, Mel said in another life he'd like to be a knight in shining armor.

"Carry a woman's scarf with you everywhere," I said. Not a scarf—a lady's favor is what I wanted to say. Favors.

"Or just a woman," he said.

"Shame on you," I said, because I thought about his hands in my chest, massaging my heart back to life. And I didn't listen as they prattled on, because I was thinking of the old couple's camper, their shampoo and snacks and medicine spilled out onto the road.

•

My new husband Nick could be my old husband what's his name. My blood had been replaced with gin—how does that feel, little heart? I never saw the baby I lost, because it was too early. I hadn't had a chance to tell my sister about it, even. Almost-auntie. At night, my empty belly lay between myself and my ex-husband. He sweat when he slept; a hot sleeper, he'd kick off my covers.

Nick was laughing with his buddy Mel, the wanna-be knight, wanna-be chef heart surgeon. Mel was bilingual—he knew the language of the heart. Ventricles and aortas and chambers. I knew only a few words, the equivalent of asking for the bathroom, how are you, where are you from? Nick and I spoke only English, and even then, I did not often understand him.

"Nothing's changed," I said.

I took another drink—here was the benefit of gin. It could be served cold.

•

I wanted Mel to finish the story. I tried to light a cigarette. It had been years since I smoked. My fingers were itchy. I couldn't get the match to light. I was clumsy like a child. Was the wind coming in through the windows, or was it Ed's heavy breathing?

There was tension between Mel and Terri, but I didn't understand it or care. It was obvious they weren't talking about love.

Nick had asked for me, but Mel ignored him.

"What happened?" Maybe I could pull the story out of him with my tongue.

He understood, because he told me if he didn't love Terri and if Nick wasn't his best friend, he'd carry me off. I would have climbed up on his horse and given all my favors to know what happened to the old couple.

Terri told him to tell his story.

Once upon a time, an old couple recovers from a terrible accident. They lie prone in separate beds, wrapped head to toe in body casts, only nose holes, eye holes, mouth holes. The doctor bends down to the old man, who is still depressed even though he and his wife have lived against the odds. The old man tells the doctor it isn't the accident, not all of it, it's that he can't see his wife through the eye holes. He can't look at her.

This is the end of the story.

Children, are you ashamed of yourselves?

Maybe because of this story, Mel wanted to call his kids.

The kids were with Mel's ex-wife, who was stealing from Mel. She lived in the house he paid for with her new boyfriend, but she'd have to marry the boyfriend before Mel could stop paying. She would not do this.

Mel wanted to murder his wife, who he used to love. How does the old couple fit into this idea?

They don't.

Ha! Ed laughed from outside the window in the form of a dog barking.

Mel said his ex-wife is allergic to bees. He said he wished she would get stung by a bunch of bees and die.

"Shame on you," I said. Everyone knows bees die when they sting someone.

Nick said something about riding into the sunset.

"What does that mean, honey?" Honey! Bees! Everything is connected like everything in the body connects to the heart—even our mouths.

"I don't think I've ever been so hungry in my life," I said. I wanted Nick to feed me with his fingers. Where were those limes?

Mel turned over his empty glass, let it clatter toward Nick. How long had they been friends? Long enough, I supposed. They loved each other.

"Gin's gone," he said, like calling it, the time of death.

Terri said, "Now what?"

In the silence I could hear Ed's heart beating outside the window, waiting for Terri to take it into her hands, squeeze it into pulp, milk it into juice, then mix it with gin for the next dinner party, and the next.

Marble Halls
after Tobias Wolff

> *The bullet is already in the brain; it won't be outrun forever, or charmed to a halt. In the end it will do its work and leave the troubled skull behind, dragging its comets tale of memory and hope and talent and love into the marble hall of commerce.*
> —Tobias Wolff, "Bullet in the Brain"

On Wednesdays, Deb went to the bank. Check her balance, take out her allotted cash for the week. After retirement, the budget was tight, but she was well able for it—she had been trained well by Samuel. Every morning of their married life, he sent her an updated worksheet of her daily expenses. She had learned to make coffee at home, bring her lunch, cut roses for the house from the garden (and sometimes her neighbor's garden, when the Volvo was missing from the driveway). Handmade cards, newspaper for giftwrapping, leftovers monitored carefully, flea markets. A sort of game, as she came to think about it over time. A dollar saved here, there. Fun, really, in a certain way—why not?

Samuel had not prepared her for the appearance of bank robbers at the bank; this, he would have dismissed as the stuff of television and novels. What would he have allotted for lost time in the line? The cost of a new pair of underwear, as she could feel now even the small wetness there? The guys even looked like they stepped straight out of the movies: their black masks on, their blue matching suits. One man with a sawed-off shotgun—she had never seen this in real life, who had? Though books and movies came from somewhere, didn't they? Real life, like she was living it now.

Jessica, whom she had known from work and was standing in line ahead of Deb, swayed a bit, and Deb reached out to steady her.

"Keep your big mouth shut!" one of the robbers said to the guard, who seemed to be praying. The robber had a gun held to the guard's neck. Deb had only seen Samuel die, and this in the hospital, with machines on. It hadn't even felt like a death at all, if Deb was to be honest.

The horrible man behind her was talking to the robber—what was he on about? "Great script, eh? The stern, brass-knuckled poetry of the dangerous classes."

His tone reminded her of Samuel, the way she had been compelled to paint her nails, to move her Nora Roberts books into the garage after a certain look, the look she saw now in the man's eyes, the rude man who sneered as if his face knew no other expression. Nora Roberts was her favorite author, the Irish Trilogy, especially, which she read and reread, Jude Murray, practical American, and the fiery Irish Gallaghers, all so good-looking. What was the harm, she wondered as she had packed up her books into leftover boxes in the garage, of a little light reading? A little diversion?

At first, she had imagined herself as Jude Murray (Deb after all was American, too), then in the third book, the fierce Darcy Gallagher, an Irish spitfire who took nothing from no one. She imagined, most likely, Darcy Gallagher would not have endured a daily budget report from Samuel. She imagined Samuel would not have ravished anyone on the ancient wooden floor of an Irish pub.

She had not told anyone this, but she had been planning for a trip to Ireland. She hoped she would not die without seeing the glowing green hills she had read about so many times; without having the inevitable affair with a wealthy and handsome Irish man, maybe a cook or a musician or a historian or a writer, someone who would feed her Irish whiskey and sing her to sleep.

What was the harm of a formula for life—hadn't Samuel wanted a formula, also? Eggs for breakfast, a light lunch (leftovers), a healthy, affordable meal, a night out to a restaurant once a month, a tidy house, ironed shirts (starched, also, by Deb), a daily report and a weekly going-over of the expenses over Sunday coffee and bagels (bagels from the deli, a great Sunday splurge). Uninspired but comfortable sex three nights per week, no children by no fault of their own ("Not in the cards," he would say about this to anyone who asked, and she wondered exactly whose deck they had been playing with), retirement at sixty-three, 401Ks, social security, appropriate life insurance, etc. etc. He had died tidily, even, in the hospital—clean and delicate, the nose hairs having been trimmed by her (Deb), Thursday morning per usual.

The formula for a Nora Roberts novel was one Deb knew and enjoyed: woman with interesting job (domestic and/or creative in some way) left by terrible man or having left terrible man, meets new man (with interesting job/talent, maybe singer or chef?), new man is interested, woman finds herself professionally/personally, woman overcomes interior conflict (childhood experience, past relationship), woman's relationship with new man threated via misunderstanding in some way (jealously, perhaps, as yet unresolved issue with aforementioned terrible man, childhood experience, etc.), woman empowered to take control of her own destiny by finally confronting said past trauma, new man reclaimed, hot sex between woman and new man with the word *member* thrown in somewhere (Deb loved that word, *member*—why is it no one used this word in real life?), ending with a happily ever after with hot sex, everyone more attractive than they arrived and also wealthier.

No nose hair trimming or budgeting involved! She imagined what Samuel would have done if she had ever mentioned to him the word *member*. "Once we finish these accounts and bagels, Samuel, I would like to wrap my mouth around your throbbing member."

She found herself giggling, a hysterical laugh bubbling upward.

Meanwhile, an exchange had been happening between the man behind her and the bank robbers. In a Nora Roberts novel, the man wouldn't have been horrible at all, but maybe would have even saved her, would have taken her home and removed her (lacey) bra slowly, with reverence.

The horrible man in line behind her was giggling himself, and Deb wondered—had the robbers released some kind of gas into the air?

"Fuck with me again, you're history. *Capeesh*?" the robber said.

The man was laughing like a lunatic—what on Earth had gotten into him? She wanted to slap him hard. Maybe it was she, Deb, who would save the man; maybe this was the plot twist? She considered Nora Roberts a feminist, really.

"I'm sorry, I'm sorry," the man was blubbering. "*Capeesh*, oh, God, *capeesh*," and the robber with the gun in his hand raised the gun and shot the horrible laughing man right in the head.

The man's blood and gore sprayed Deb in the face, and in that moment, she thought of Samuel's neat death under the hospital sheet. She heard when people die, there's an embarrassing expulsion of gas and shit and urine, but she hadn't experienced this with Samuel; maybe there had been something done beforehand, or maybe she hadn't noticed? The kind nurse had held her hand, just as Jessica whom she had known from work held her hand now, and she thought, plot twist, maybe she would go home with Jessica instead. Maybe Jessica would wipe her face clean of the blood with a warm washcloth, and then, compelled by Deb's clean, soft skin, be moved to kiss her there, on that soft cheek. Maybe Jessica would undo her messy bun and let her brown hair fall to her shoulders, and maybe she would run her fingers through Deb's own short curly blond hair, which Deb cut herself to save a weekly cost at the salon, which Jessica would find charming and practical, and maybe Jessica would lie Deb back on the couch gently, and Jessica's mouth would be warm against Deb. No members allowed! Deb wanted to giggle again, but she was afraid to open her mouth, as blood or something worse might trickle in there, and then she would be able to kiss no one nor taste anything else for the rest of her life, even the hot taste of an Irish whiskey.

Deb did not remember the hot California summers in the valley, or how when the skies were pink, her dad would say, "Earthquake weather." The pretty sunset ruined by the fear of the ground opening up and swallowing them all, her beautiful mother who would die when Deb was seventeen years old, her little brother who lived now in Wisconsin with a woman who made scarves and other things she sold on Etsy under the handle "DeckYoNeck." Her father in a nursing home for years and years with Alzheimer's thinking Deb was her own mother, saying things like, "Take me out of here, doll, I'll make it worth your while." The teacher who had asked her to stay after class and instead breathed hot down her blouse while something hard poked her in the back. The clean smell of chlorine in the pool where she swam again and again away from that teacher, the feeling of the hard thing. Her boyfriend who pulled her pants up over her little belly after they ate pizza, saying, "Here, let me help you with this." The neighbor who had brought over blueberry pancakes when Deb had been ill, telling her about how her husband had freed the concentration camps during the war, what he had seen. Samuel saying, "It's not in the cards" while she cried and cried in the hospital parking lot. Dropping an entire book in the bathtub and fishing it out again, reading it anyway, the pages drying thicker and the book bending wide with time. Girl meets boy, girl loses boy, girl gets boy back, girl gets herself. Her father gone, her beautiful mother gone, her brother wrapped head to toe in crocheted scarves, FaceTiming from the snow: "We miss you, Deb, come visit any time!" Her best friend from childhood: "I hate you, Deb, you're a bitch." Her first boyfriend proposing; the distinct pleasure of telling him, "No, thank you." Samuel's heaving chest as she lay there after lovemaking, his hand running down her back, wondering if she could work her magic and make them something from the cupboard for dinner? She could do that, she had thought then, she could work her magic. She had made something from nothing, something that nourished them both.

Nora Roberts knew books could not begin with the beginning of the marriage; Deb knew that as well. Which was why this time in her life was so exciting. Samuel's ending was her beginning. The terrible man had left her. Deb knew what would happen next; this is how Nora Roberts made all her money, some of which had been Deb's (cash).

The blood was drying and she could feel it tighten like one of those homemade skin peels she had made from a recipe on the internet. Would her pores be revealed smaller? Would Jessica be drawn to Deb's newly made bright skin?

This is what she remembered. Cool. An open window. Endless sky, traffic buzzing, her mother leaning against the wall painted yellow as Deb pleads for her to think of roses. No other reason presents itself to Deb, in this moment. Think of roses! Deb looks on as her mother considers the sky. In a movie, she thinks, the moment would slow down to a ridiculous sense of pause, her mother climbing into the window, Deb herself reaching out, her mother gazing back with a romantic look (it would have to be romantic, wouldn't it, in the movies?), eyes glazed with madness or peace, her mother's dress billowing as she falls, slowly, from the sixth floor window on the busy street in Sherman Oaks, California, her dark hair long, streaming behind as everyone watches, Deb, her neighbors, the boys a bit down the road playing baseball, pausing bat, gloves mid-air, dust in tufts at their feet, molecules of dust suspended, mouths opening, fingers pointing. In a Nora Roberts story, this would be enough for Deb to have to overcome; this would make for the reveal during which Deb, disclosing this moment from her past, becomes close to the new man, who will take her away to the crumbling castle in Ireland he has inherited and which Deb will help him rebuild.

    The bank robbers have continued their work, the blood has seeped into Deb's mouth, in spite of her lips closed tight, there is no keeping it out—the terrible man's exploded head, lost of all stories and secrets lived and read for good. This can't be helped. But for now, Deb can still make time. Time for her mother's shoe to fall gently into the hibiscus where later, a little girl will pluck it like a flower, time for the curtains to close behind her mother in the wind, their lace delicate in the late pink sunset light that had, in fact, correctly predicted the earth's shift, time for the boys in the baseball field to pick up where they'd left off, smack their fists into their dirty mitts, whisper words to each other Deb will never know, never hear, never understand.

Miss Emily, Poor Emily
after William Faulkner

> *We did not say she was crazy then. We believed she had to do that. We remembered all the young men her father had driven away, and we knew that with nothing left, she would have to cling to that which had robbed her, as people will.*
> —William Faulkner, "A Rose for Emily"

When painting porcelain: Overglaze painting can be forgiving; as with watercolor, one can erase mistakes.

When painting porcelain: Floral designs are pleasing to the eye. I prefer magnolia, lily, lilac, and rose.

When Papa dies: I draw a crayon portrait of him from memory. Papa was a strong man, tall and lean. He did not believe in waste or indulgence. He wanted only the best for me, his daughter, would not abide for men lesser-than in class or appearance or taste. John, he sent away for misuse of the cutlery. Phillip, for his horse (unkempt). Elliot, lack of manners (laughing too loud at dinner, food stuck in teeth). Montgomery, his mother had a large birthmark on her face. What if that passed on? Papa shuddered to think of it, and I had nightmares of stained children and dogs for seven months. Papa! So careful with me.

When Papa dies, I am not sure he is dead. His eyes are open, for one, and for another, there is a feeling that he is still breathing. I hear it, even though when I go into the room where we have him laid out, Tobe says I must be dreaming. He doesn't say crazy. Tobe says he's been watching Papa, and there is no breathing from a dead man. He says I am hearing the wind, that I should sleep.

It seems a daughter's duty, if no one else (!), to be sure her father is dead before he is buried. Think of how he might be betrayed, waking up in a box in the cold earth. Think of his great regret, his disappointment. After all his care.

In the crayon portrait, I draw him breathing as I heard it the night he died: steady, with purpose.

When painting porcelain: Do not use crayon.

Papa leaves me the house, as he promised. A beautiful house, belonging to our family for a long time in the way things are done. From its windows, I look out upon the town and imagine the stories of the people below, their children and love affairs. Sometimes, I paint their stories onto the porcelain, like I've seen done with stories of the Saints, their lives unfolding one stained-glass window at a time.

I do not lack for an artistic life. Papa's crayon portrait, for example, keeps me very busy. I have not yet got his eyes right. I have not yet heard the portrait breathe as I have drawn it to do.

They want to take Papa's body away; I want to be sure before they do. How can anyone be sure? I have often mistaken the dog's sleep for death. I have often felt the panic in my throat at the dog's still form. What of Papa's long sleep? What if he is simply suspended in a dream?

Do not come in. This is my house.

Mine. Doesn't the land mean something anymore? Go away, do not come in.

Dear Papa, are you breathing? Papa, do you like your portrait? Have I captured your expression? Am I making you proud?

I am sick; I have a fever. When painting porcelain, I paint instead Papa's crayon portrait. His eyes are still open—why do they make me give him up? He is my Papa, I am his Emily. What business of theirs? When Auntie died, they clucked like old hens. Auntie was crazy, they all said, but Papa said she was the way she was because of her grief, because her sons, his cousins, had all died. Accidents, sicknesses. It happened all the time to mothers, he said. Papa knew. He said, watch how they try to take everything from her. And they did! Her money and house. It is a dangerous thing, to grieve.

It is so warm from my fever! In a fit, I have cut my hair from my neck. How cool it feels! How light and free. Papa would not approve, but he is dead now, and away from here.

It takes no time at all in the morning to prepare myself; I am often painting porcelain by first light.

I am painting porcelain with new tools: an imprint of a leaf from the garden, strands of my own hair. Papa's fine tooth comb. Tobe says it's my finest work yet!

If only I had made an urn for Papa, if only they had let me keep him. He is buried now, and I have no way of putting him into a pot I have decorated just for him. Designs both practical and bold: triangles, and an image of the house, which I am so grateful for—the house like a friend to me in this friendless town. I look from its windows as I look out my own eyes. Its body a body for my body. I often do not leave the house for days. Tobe is well and able for the shopping.

A new man has arrived: Homer Barron. The name of a hero in a book. His voice is so loud in the house! His arms so wide, he reminds me of a horse! He watches me paint and comments on my style and invention. He does not paint himself, though his light eyes are those of an artist.

I am glad Papa is not in the urn; Papa would not approve of Homer as he would not approve of my hair. (Homer likes my hair, he says it is "daring.") Sometimes, I hear Papa breathing again after Homer has left.

Sometimes, I turn Papa's crayon portrait toward the wall. I am a grown woman! With my own home. What woman these days can make such a claim?

Homer kisses warmly and with intention. I find myself out of breath when smelling his cigar smoke. I like to inhale it. I can smell it on my clothes after he has left, and I keep the clothes on through the night, to keep the smell in my nose.

This must be love.

Why does the town torment us so? It is their fault Homer does not ask me to marry him. He says the south is too old in its ways. Perverse. He does not want to rush.

He is a modern man. He encourages me to experiment with my art. Tells loud jokes. Has many friends.

I hear the town whisper about me from my window. Do they know I watch them like a god? I have become furniture to them. They do not care what I hear or see.

Homer! When he touches me, I look out my own eyes.

This interfering place: they have sent for my cousins. Two women like reeds—the wind blows through them with a scream. They sit while Homer visits with me. Sentinels. They make noises in their throats like dying birds when he takes out his cigars.

Homer, do not listen to these cousins! Do not leave me to link arms with your lovely friends. Do not leave me alone with these women who look at me and see the value of this dinner plate, that china cup. They have no interest in painting or art. I often confuse them; I wonder do they swap faces at night.

The cousins snore from their rooms, and I do not sleep. Homer is out with his friends. He says he does not want to see the cousins. I do not want to see the cousins.

One laughs at my hair. The other mutters to herself as she walks around the house. They are truly crazy, they are not mothers, there is no reason for their muttering. They do not like to discuss the moon or Papa. They call Tobe names and he stays in the kitchen mostly. At night, I curse them. I draw their deaths on the porcelain: oleander blossoms. They drink from the painted cups and do not understand why I smile at them.

Of course, I know rat poison is for rats. Of course, I will not pay taxes; Papa has loaned the city money, and for this, they owe me. I will not pay their bills. I will buy poison when poison is needed.

Homer does not drink from porcelain, and therefore, I buy him a toilet set with his initials. H.B. Homer Barron! His name is like his arms, like the strong smell of his smoke. I buy him clothing Papa would have approved of; Homer is too casual from his work in construction, and he will need a nice outfit for our wedding. I will teach him what he needs to know, how to live in this house, which requires a price to be paid.

Homer! Such a man, no knowledge of flowers at all, or what they could mean when ringed around a teacup and saucer. Oleander, belladonna. What a pleasure is knowledge, when exercised with wit and attention.

Not the marrying kind!

There is another Emily—she is dead now. She, too, is an artist. We understand our houses to be shells and skins. We understand the air outside is full of poison and foes.

Like a worn bird of passage left behind
Wounded, and sinking, by its faithless kind . . .

Kind. Did she mean to write "kin"?

Mother gone forever—had she even existed at all? Papa, buried perhaps while breathing. Oh, that he should think I had betrayed him! Or worse, that I had been careless.

At night, I cuddle into Homer and light my own cigar. I smoke it down in bed. I cannot give them up, not when I have become so dependent.

My hair turns gray in one night. I love it. Homer might call it "daring." Perhaps it is all the smoke! I look more like Papa now, which is a comfort.

Homer does not dream; he is a man and his body is worn from physical labor and all that loud laughing.

The clothes fit him perfectly. I make sure his collar is straight. His nightgown, also, is the perfect length. I know him so well.

They think I do not see them creeping around my house at night! Let them sprinkle curses on me. They don't know what guards I have set, what traps. They do not look up to see me see.

If it smells so bad, just light a cigar!

Homer! His hands are large, covering my stomach at night.

A soft and safe feeling, his large hands on my thin stomach.

I do not eat much.

I am feeling well again; I invite students to learn to paint porcelain. They admire what I have done. I show them my collection, and they call out names of flowers like prayers. The other Emily likes hyacinths, lily of the valley, peonies. Peonies, with heads hanging low, too heavy for their bodies.

> *A solemn thing – it was – I said –*
> *A Woman – White – to be –*
> *And wear – if God should count me fit –*
> *Her blameless mystery –*

Poems can also be painted onto porcelain. I like to follow a line around a cup.

At night, Homer comforts me as I smoke a cigar. We are growing old! I laugh. Look how our skin has aged. Homer is so in love, he refuses to leave our bed at all. I read him poems.

That night when the cousins had gone, I had prepared for Homer a welcome-home banquet. I offered him my body, which was my body and also the house. I offered him the toilet set, the clothing. The nightgown. This was a language I was speaking, a language of things.

He did not understand, not being one of us, after all. Papa would have known, but he was in no place to speak.

The children bring their paints and brushes. They are excited to learn. The other Emily liked children, too, I read. But no children of her own. Nothing, then, to drive her crazy. More time for her poems, her garden. Poor Emily, alone in her house! What comfort Homer is at night—I do not know what I would do without him.

My art has long since evolved from Papa's crayon portrait, but I leave the portrait downstairs anyway, to remind myself how far I've come.

I am now older than Papa was when he died. This math does not make sense to me, but then again, I suspect this is not math at all, but poetry.

The children tire me so with their questions. I caught one heading upstairs, and she didn't even say she was sorry. Privacy and ownership! Papa would not approve of these children's manners.

Sometimes I dream of churches, of stained glass windows telling stories of death and torment. How did I find them so charming before? I had seen only the lessons of faith. I had forgotten about the bodies. Hairshirts. Whips. Homer had carried a horsewhip once. He had not been afraid to use it. He has taught me many lessons.

There is hair on my shirt, but it is my own, and it causes me no pain. It is the gray of dust, of dusk. It glints in the sunlight like metal. I do not use the color gray when I paint porcelain. There is no flower colored gray in my gardens.

Tobe and I speak in the language of things. Groceries. He sweeps dust. We watch each other's eyes. He is my longest companion. We have never touched.

I am dizzy for two days. My heart flutters like one of Emily's butterflies; it is a funny feeling, holding my breath, but I am not holding it, my chest is empty for a while in the strange spaces between my heartbeats. Papa's face appears in those spaces. Emily's words.

Futile – the winds –
To a heart in port –
Done with the compass –
Done with the chart!

Poor Emily, alone in the end as I am not, my head close to my love's, his body my bed my body my house my family my Grierson my Homer Barron Emily Barron, Barren, Bare, Wren, Singing Emily, Emily.

Women in windows, looking out at history.

Jennifer Murvin is the author of two story collections, *She Says* (Small Harbor Publishing) and *Real California Living* (forthcoming Braddock Avenue Books). Her essays, stories, and graphic narratives have appeared in literary journals such as *Hayden's Ferry Review*, *River Styx*, *The Southampton Review*, *The Pinch*, *december magazine*, *DIAGRAM*, *The Florida Review*, *Catamaran Literary Reader*, *Indiana Review*, *CutBank*, *Post Road*, *American Short Fiction* (Winner of the American Short(er) Fiction Contest, judged by Stuart Dybek), *Phoebe*, *The Sun*, *Mid-American Review*, *Midwestern Gothic*, and *Cincinnati Review*. Jen is an Assistant Professor of English at Missouri State University, a faculty member at the Solstice Low-Residency MFA in Creative Writing at Lasell University, and a faculty leader for the nonprofit community writing workshop River Pretty Writers Retreat. She holds an MFA in Creative Writing from Pacific University. Jen is also the owner of the indie bookstore Pagination Bookshop in Springfield, MO. Find more at https://www.jennifermurvin.com

About Small Harbor Publishing

Small Harbor Publishing is a 501c3 nonprofit organization. Our goal is to publish unique and diverse voices. We are a feminist press, and we are committed to diversity and inclusion. We strive to bring new voices to a devoted and expanding readership.

Small Harbor Publishing began in 2018 with the first issue of *Harbor Review*. The magazine is an online space where poetry and art converse. *Harbor Review* quickly grew and now publishes reviews and runs multiple micro chapbook competitions, including the Washburn Prize and the Editor's Prize.

In July 2020, Small Harbor Publishing was officially incorporated and began Harbor Editions. Harbor Editions accepts submissions through a chapbook open reading period, a hybrid chapbook open reading period, the Marginalia Series, and the Laureate Prize.

In 2023, Harbor Anthologies began with a mission to promote texts that explore social justice issues and highlight marginalized writers.

If you would like to support Small Harbor Publishing, visit our "About" page: smallharborpublishing.com/about.

www.ingramcontent.com/pod-product-compliance
Lightning Source LLC
LaVergne TN
LVHW092058060526
838201LV00047B/1456